Twinsikins

True Tales Of Twin Tails

The First "Tail"

Liz and Ralph Kennedy

illustrated by Michelle Maul

Copyright © 2010 by Liz and Ralph Kennedy and Twin Clydes, LLC
ISBN-10: 1450561640
EAN-13: 9781450561648
LCCN: 2010901590

www.TwinClydes.com

Illustrated by Michelle Maul

Midge and Myrtle would like to thank the many people who helped make this story possible!

We could not have done this without you. The list of people that helped us with this is so long we can't list everyone individually. From our everyday barn help to our occasional advice givers, THANK YOU!

Special thanks to all of the Twinsikins Fan Club members. Thank you for your support and interest in Midge and Myrtle's great adventures.

Claudia Clydesdale was worried. Her people were moving away and could not take her with them. She stood in the rain, munching her hay and worried. Where would she live? What would happen when her baby came? Who would take care of them?

Claudia had a nice big barn where she felt safe. Would her new home have a safe spot for her? She would miss her barnyard friends. She hoped there would be other animals at her new home. She had always been the only horse on the farm, but she enjoyed the company of the chickens and cows. Maybe, if she was lucky, she would go to a farm with other horses!

Later that day, a truck pulling a horse trailer drove into the yard. One of Claudia's owners came out of the house and talked with the people who came in the truck with the horse trailer. Soon, her owner brought Claudia to meet the new people.

"Hello, Claudia. It's nice to meet you!" said Liz.

"Snort!" said Claudia.

"Hello, big girl!" said Ralph.

"Snort!" said Claudia.

Claudia's owner handed her lead rope to Liz while Ralph scratched Claudia's neck. "You are a very beautiful horse!" said Ralph.

"Snort!" said Claudia.

A short time later, the new people opened up the trailer and loaded Claudia into it. Claudia knew about trailers, but she still worried. Where was she going? Were these nice people? Would she stay with them or would they take her to other people? Would the new place be nice for her baby when it came?

Claudia worried about all of these things while they rolled down the driveway and out of the yard. After awhile, it got dark outside and still they rolled on. The people would stop every now and then, and offer Claudia water and hay to munch on.

"These must be nice people," Claudia thought.

Just when Claudia was getting sleepy, the truck and trailer stopped again. This time, Claudia could hear and smell other horses. "Welcome to your new home!" called Liz and Ralph.

They unloaded Claudia from the trailer and walked her into the barn. They gave her the biggest stall in the barn, as well as more hay and fresh, cold water. The stall was clean, dry and warm. There were other horses across the hall and also next to her. Claudia stopped worrying so much. She was tired.

"Good night! See you in the morning!" whispered Liz and Ralph, as they shut off the lights.
Soon Claudia went to sleep.

When morning came, the nice people named Liz and Ralph came back and gave Claudia and the other horses their breakfast and put them out in the pastures for the day. Claudia went outside with some of the girl horses. Some of them were nice to her, and some were not so nice. They didn't bother Claudia too much because she was so much bigger than they were.

It wasn't too long before Claudia made friends with another horse named Sister. "I'm going to have a baby," Claudia told Sister.

"Me, too!" Sister said. "We can be mommies together!" The two friends were very happy.

Claudia was not worried anymore; in fact, she was very happy. She had good hay and water all the time. Liz and Ralph brought her grain everyday. She was brushed and patted and loved all the time. She was very happy to have her new friend Sister, too.

Winter soon came and Claudia's tummy grew bigger as her baby grew inside. When spring was just a month away, Liz and Ralph moved her into a new stall. It was even bigger than her old stall. They made it especially for Claudia and her baby. She liked it very much.

One evening, just as spring was arriving, Claudia felt funny in her tummy. She was in her new stall, and Liz and Ralph had done chores and gone to the house for the night. She tried not to worry, but it wasn't getting any better. In fact, it was getting worse! She was starting to sweat and breathe hard, when all of a sudden she knew what was happening.

The baby was coming!

Where were Liz and Ralph? She did not know what to do! She was very uncomfortable. Claudia lay down on her side, which felt a little better. Suddenly, she had a big pain in her tummy and then Whoosh! Her baby came out quick as a flash. Just then, Liz and Ralph quietly came into the barn.

They were very proud of Claudia and very happy to see the baby! Liz and Ralph talked softly and reassured Claudia, who was very glad they were there. Liz checked on Claudia while Ralph dried off the foal.

"We are going to call you Myrtle," Ralph said to the foal.

"You are going to be a good mommy," Liz said to Claudia.

Claudia's tummy still felt funny, but she did not know how to tell Liz and Ralph. She got up and walked around the stall and sniffed at her baby.

She lay back down near her foal, and her tummy gave her another big pain.

When Ralph looked at her hind end, he stopped what he was doing and stared. "Liz, come and look at this!" said Ralph.

"Oh no!" said Liz. "This never happens!"

They saw another pair of hooves. Claudia was having another baby! Liz grabbed the tiny little hooves and pulled! Sure enough, there was another baby! After making sure the foal was alive and breathing, she ran to call the veterinarian.

While Liz was on the phone, Ralph began drying off the second foal. She was very, very small – especially for a Clydesdale. She was not even half the size of her sister.

When Liz got off the phone, she said, "We have to make sure that she doesn't sound gurgley when she breathes."

Liz and Ralph listened to her nose and chest while the tiny horse breathed. "She sounds gurgley to me", said Liz.

"What do we do?" asked Ralph.

"Dr. Rabb said to lift her hind end over a gate so the fluid can drain out of her lungs," explained Liz.

Since there wasn't a gate nearby, Ralph spun a towel into a rope and lifted her little hind end up high in the air while Liz patted her on the sides. After a few seconds, the little horse gave a big cough and a whole bunch of fluid came out of her tiny little nose. She was breathing much better already!

"What should we call her?" Ralph asked.

"Let's call her 'Midget' because she's so small," Liz replied.

Claudia was back on her feet and feeling much better. Although Myrtle was on her feet a few minutes after she was born, Midget wasn't even trying yet. Just when Liz and Ralph were starting to worry again, she began trying to get up. No matter how hard she tried she was just too weak to do it.

Myrtle was now nursing from Claudia. Liz and Ralph picked up Midgie (as they were now calling her) and stood her on her feet. She was very wobbly, but managed to stay up on her feet. They helped her over to Claudia, but she was so little that she could not reach high enough to nurse.

"We will have to bottle feed her until she is big enough to nurse on her own." said Liz.

"How often does she need to eat?" asked Ralph.

"Every hour" Liz answered. "Hopefully soon she will grow bigger."

Liz went to the closet and brought back a big bottle and filled it halfway with Claudia's milk. Once Midgie figured out how to drink from the bottle, she ate very well. She was hungry!

Soon after the twins were done with their first meal, they grew very sleepy. Myrtle lay down near the wall of their stall and Midgie wandered over and lay down next to her sister. Claudia was exhausted and sleeping standing up. Just as Liz and Ralph were about to leave them alone to sleep for a little while, Liz noticed that Midgie was shivering.

"Maybe we should take her temperature," Liz said, going to get a thermometer.

"That's a good idea," said Ralph.

"She's a little under normal temperature," Liz reported. "She could probably use a blanket, but I don't think I have one small enough."

Liz quickly ran to the upper barn and sorted through all of her horse blankets. "Darn! None of these are even close to fitting Midgie."

"What about one of the dogs' winter coats?" Ralph wondered.

"Let's get one and see if it fits!" said Liz.

Sure enough, the dog coat fit Midgie just right. "It's a good thing for Midgie that we have big dogs and not little ones!" laughed Liz.

Now Midgie was warm and comfortable. Midgie and Myrtle were sleeping side by side in the warm, clean straw with Claudia watching over them.

"Let's get some sleep, too," said Ralph.

"Yes," said Liz. "We will have to come back again soon to feed Midgie!"

Liz and Ralph took turns all night going to the barn and checking on Claudia and Myrtle, and feeding Midgie. In the morning, they went down together to feed all the horses, clean the stalls, and wait for Dr. Rabb to come and do examinations on the twins.

"How are they doing?" he asked, getting out of his truck.

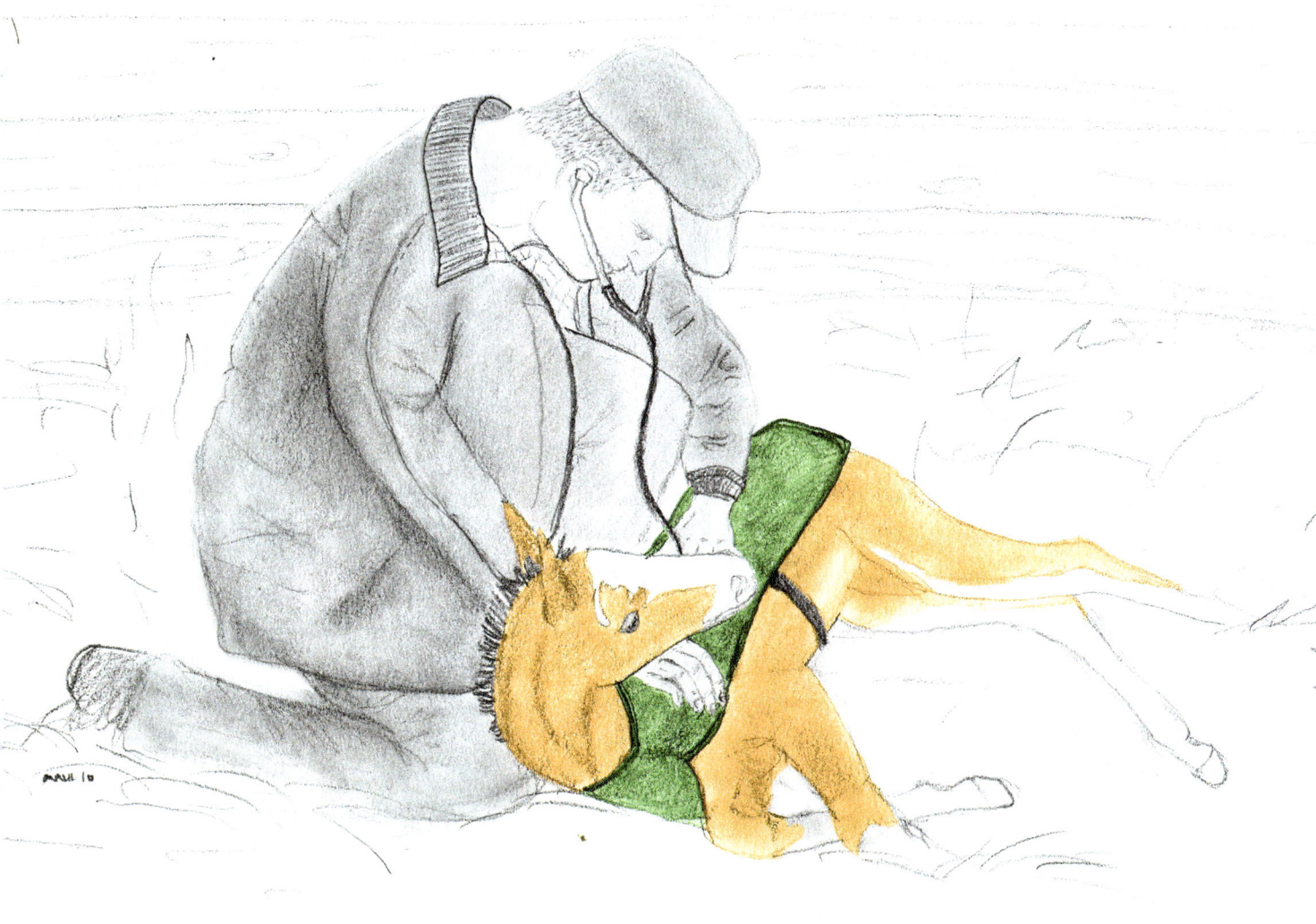

"Well," said Liz, "Myrtle is nursing just fine, but she keeps sweating on and off. Midgie can't seem to figure out how to get up on her own and we are bottle feeding her because she is too little to reach Claudia to nurse."

"Well, let's take a look at them!" said Dr. Rabb.

The three people went into the stall with Claudia and her babies. Dr. Rabb examined all three horses. When he was finished, all three of them walked out of the stall, and Dr. Rabb gave Liz and Ralph his diagnosis.

"Claudia is fine," he began, "but the twins each have their own problems. Myrtle has an irregular heartbeat, which she will probably grow out of.

I suspect that is what is causing her sweating on and off. Midgie has a strong, normal heartbeat and her lungs sound good. However, as weak as she is, and still not standing on her own, she may only live a few days at most. If she lives until she is two weeks old her chances will increase."

"Oh no!" cried Liz and Ralph together. They were very upset.

"I will come back and check on them next week, hopefully," said Dr. Rabb.

"Yes, please do!" Liz and Ralph said.

After Dr. Rabb left, Liz and Ralph went to the farmhouse and got on the computer and began to research twin births in horses. They found that horses do occasionally have twins, but they found very few twins that had actually survived. No matter how hard they looked they could not find any help on what to do.

"Well," said Liz, "I guess we will keep doing what we have been doing and hope for the best!"

For the next 10 days, Liz and Ralph fed Midgie every hour. Each time they fed her they would have to stand her up and give her the bottle. Midgie always ate very well. On the 11th day, Liz was heading to the little pasture near the barn where they went during the day, and was shocked at what she saw!

"Midgie!" cried Liz. "You got up all by yourself!!!"

Sure enough, Midgie was standing for the first time on her own! She had walked around before, but she had always needed help getting on her feet.

Her legs were long, and her body was so short, along with being so weak that she could never get her legs under her properly to have the strength to get up. Now here she was standing up all by herself! Myrtle had been on her feet by herself before she was an hour old and now – finally – Midgie could do it, too! Liz and Ralph were so proud of her, they just about cried with joy.

When the twins were 3 weeks old, Midgie learned how to drink her formula from a bucket. By the time she was 6 weeks old, she had grown so much that she could nurse from Claudia.

Myrtle still had the sweats every day, but was otherwise just fine. She ran and played and was very curious about everything. Now that Midgie was stronger, she had a playmate, too!

Claudia was very happy – and proud! Both of her daughters were doing well and she was very protective of them.

Shortly after Midge could start getting herself up, Claudia's friend Sister had her baby. His name was Jack, and he was a beautiful Appaloosa foal with spots on his rump.

Jack was a big baby. He was only 1 day old and already as tall as Myrtle. Even though Jack was almost a whole month younger than Midge and Myrtle, he grew taller faster, but the twins continued to grow and grow and grow. When they were three months old, the twins had another exam from Dr. Rabb. He checked them all over and was glad to say that they were doing just fine. Midgie was growing stronger every day, and Myrtle's heartbeat was much more regular, and she was hardly ever sweaty anymore.

As the twins grew, word about the "Clydesdale twins" spread. Every day, more and more people came to see them. A lot of people brought cameras and took pictures. One day a newspaper man came by to talk to Liz and take some pictures. The next day, they were on the front page of the local newspaper. The following day, a man from the local TV channel came and did a story on the twins. They were on the 6 p.m. and 11 p.m. news, as well as on the morning report the next day. The television reporter liked them so much that he came back to visit the twins (and Liz and Ralph) often.

Now that Midgie was big enough to nurse from Claudia, Liz and Ralph moved them to a new pasture a little further from the barn. It was a big, grassy pasture with plenty of room to run and play. Midgie soon discovered that she loved to run. Several times a day, she would zoom around the pasture as fast as fast could be! With her smaller and lighter body, she was faster than Myrtle. Myrtle liked to run fast, too, but Midgie was faster.

Soon Sister and Jack came to share the pasture. Midgie tried to impress Jack with her speed, but Jack just laughed at her! That made Midgie very mad. When Midgie was running her very fastest,

Jack just zoomed right past her, and he wasn't even trying! Midgie was heartbroken. She wasn't the fastest horse anymore. Claudia tried to cheer her up. "You are still the fastest Clydesdale! Besides, draft horses are bred for size and strength, not speed. Jack's breed is known for going fast and jumping high. Each breed has a purpose, and neither one is better than the other. One day, you'll be a big, beautiful horse with your own special job!"

Midgie felt a little better, though she worried that she wouldn't be good for anything because she was so small. More than anything, she wanted to be the best at something!

In the middle of summer, there was a lot of activity around the farm. The barns were being painted, and flowers and shrubs were being planted. Grass was mowed, trees pruned, and everything was washed and cleaned. The twins watched all of this with great interest. "What is going on?" they wondered.

One day, a big truck pulled up to the farm and some men got out. They talked with Liz and Ralph for a few minutes and then began to set up a huge tent. "What is that for?" wondered the twins. That night they found out what all the fuss was about.

Liz and Ralph were going to get married at the farm, AND, the twins were going to be the flower girls! They were very excited and happy. They could hardly sleep that night. When they finally drifted off to sleep, they dreamed of how exciting being the "flower fillies" was going to be!

The Tail End

Read all about Midge and Myrtle's exciting appearance as "Flower Fillies" at Liz and Ralph's wedding in their second Tail.

Visit TwinClydes.com often for Twinsikins news and information and release date of the second Tail.

Myrtle

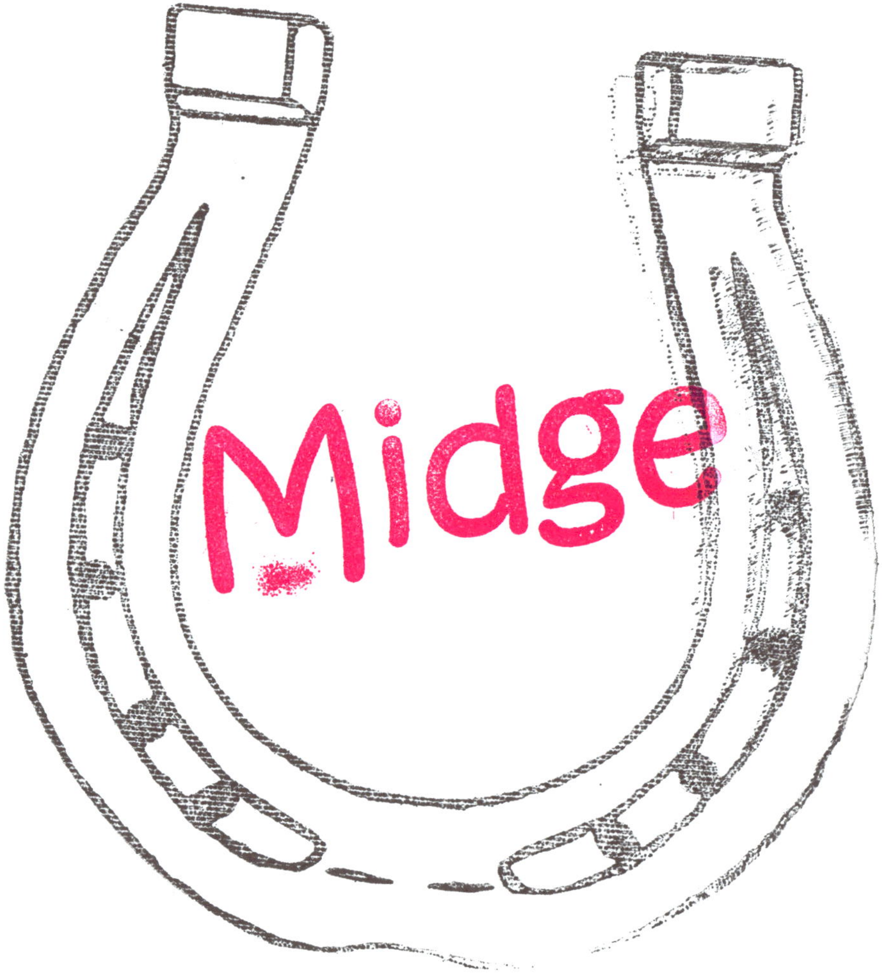
Midge

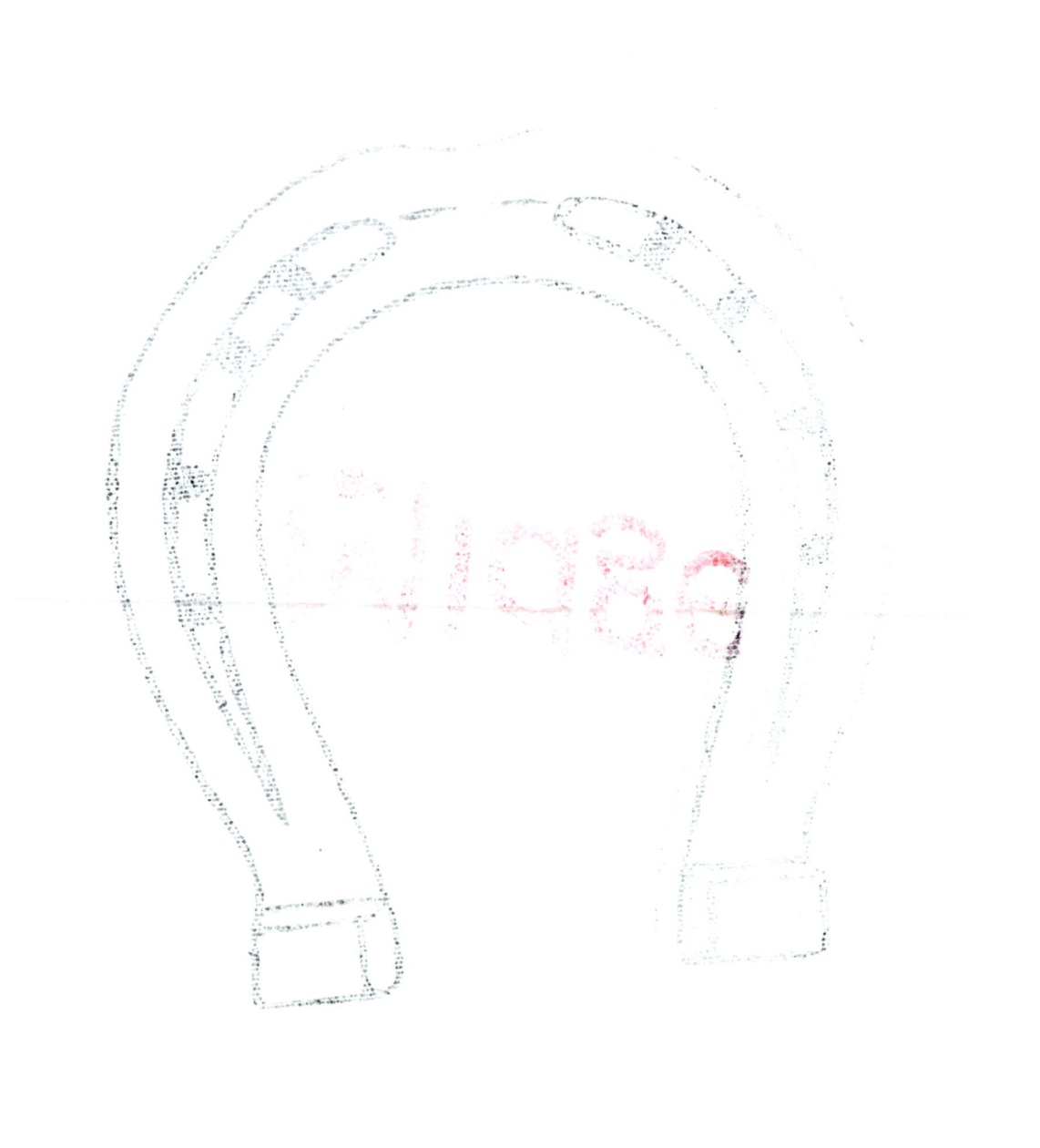

Made in the USA
Charleston, SC
09 November 2010